TAX
EFFICIENT WEALTH

TAX EFFICIENT WEALTH

THE BLUEPRINT TO QUICKLY BUILD TAX-EFFICIENT WEALTH TO ACHIEVE FINANCIAL FREEDOM IN FOUR ACTIONABLE STEPS

KEN GREEN, CPA CA, MBA

Copyright © 2020 Ken Green, CPA CA, MBA

Publishing Services by Happy Self Publishing
www.happyselfpublishing.com

Year: 2020

All rights reserved. No reproduction, transmission or copy of this publication can be made without the written consent of the author in accordance with the provision of the Copyright Acts. Any person doing so will be liable to civil claims and criminal prosecution.

Happy Self Publishing.

BOOK OUTLINE

PRAISE 7

INTRODUCTION 11

CHAPTER 1: THE FOUNDATION—WHAT YOU
NEED TO KNOW 13
   Marginal Tax Rates 14
   Different Tax Rates for Different Types of Income .. 17
   Tax Credits vs. Tax Deductions 18
   Tax-Deferred vs. Tax-Free 21
   The Three Powerful Accelerators 23

CHAPTER 2: THE OBSTACLES 31
   Taxes 32
   Nondeductible Interest 33
   Cash Flow Crunch 35
   Inflation 37

CHAPTER 3: THE TAX-SMART PLAN 41
   Eliminate or Reduce Taxes 42
   Convert Nondeductible Interest to
   Deductible Interest 46
   Increase Cash Flow 48

CHAPTER 4: THE TOOLS 51
   Tax-Free Savings Account 52
   Registered Retirement Savings Plan 54

Registered Education Savings Plan 57
Real Estate (Primary Residence and Rental
Properties) 59
Business 61
Tax-Exempt Life Insurance 62

CHAPTER 5: THE BLUEPRINT 67
Stage 1—Save Tax Efficiently 68
Stage 2—Invest/Leverage/Grow Tax Efficiently 70
Stage 3—Invest/Leverage/Grow Tax Efficiently
with Velocity 72
Stage 4—Invest/Leverage/Grow Tax Efficiently
with 10X Velocity 74
Stage 5—Withdraw Tax-Free 76

CHAPTER 6: THE IMPLEMENTATION 79
Action Step 1—Vision 80
Action Step 2—Belief 84
Action Step 3—Assess 88
Action Step 4—Execute 96

ABOUT THE AUTHOR 103

THANK YOU ! 105

PRAISE

"I'm completely sold on this book and the incredible value it brings to readers! I've known Ken for many years and have benefited from his wealth of business insights and tax advice for several years, which have saved me thousands of dollars. As a CPA myself, I have had the opportunity to read a lot of books on finance and taxes; most of them spend pages to get to one worthwhile idea. This book is insightful, practical, and provides a comprehensive blueprint to save on taxes and build wealth. This book delivers value to its readers instantly!"

– **Wesley Ogude (MBA Queen's, CPA), CEO, Springwells Group of Companies**

"If your focus is on long-term growth of your wealth, this book is for you. Not only does Ken provide a great background information on taxes and strategies for saving on taxes, he also provides a step-by-step blueprint for changing you and your family's financial fortune. For the first time, Ken provides an intentional road map to build wealth in a tax-efficient manner. This is a must read for all those serious about building long-term wealth."

– *Nick Karadza,* **Rock Star Real Estate Brokerage**

"The secrets of wealth building can seem out of reach for middle-class and new Canadians. However, if you are ready to create wealth, do it in a structured way, AND save time and taxes, then I strongly recommend this book. This book is a tremendous resource that will not only educate you but also get you motivated to take action on your financial well-being. Thank you, Ken for this amazing gift to Canadians!"

– *Lianne Hannaway,*
CPA, CA & Founder, Wealthnuvo.com

"A simple but also thoughtful, provocative, and powerful book where Ken unravels our complicated tax laws and issues, and puts them into very understandable and applicable principles that do work. It's a refreshing read where Ken even suggests that we need to be "excited about our taxes." Our finances can be life changing and we need to embrace it. This book will change the way you think about your finances and encourage you to start now."

– *Stephen Ostapchuk,* **Agent, Desjardins Insurance**

"I found the book extremely clear and concise, with an excellent road map to managing one's finances throughout life. The goal management techniques given at the end were an added bonus."

— *Brian Clouse*

"Whether you're a salaried employee, self-employed, or a business owner, this book will provide you with tremendous insight on how you can build and accelerate your wealth over the long term. Ken brings a unique perspective as a professional Tax Advisor, Real Estate Investor, and Business Owner and lays out a road map on how you can plan your affairs to build tax-efficient wealth."

— *Tom Karadza,* **Rock Star Real Estate Brokerage**

"*TAX-EFFICIENT WEALTH* is an invaluable read for those looking to build wealth. It helps lay the foundation, so that you have the tools and knowledge you need to follow in the footsteps of the rich and successful on your way to financial freedom."

— *Sean Cooper,* **Bestselling Author of Burn Your Mortgage and Mortgage Broker**

INTRODUCTION

Income inequality is real, and the gap between the rich and the poor is growing every year. According to the St. Louis Federal Reserve, the bottom 50% of the world's population, amounting to nearly four billion people, are worth a total of $1.3 trillion. According to Forbes magazine, the top twenty billionaires in the world have a combined net worth of over $1.31 trillion, which means that the top twenty people in the world are worth more than the bottom half of the entire world combined. This is simply mind-blowing!

The stats in America and Canada are similar with the richest 1% controlling approximately 50% of the entire national wealth, the next 19% (middle class) controlling approximately 43% and the poorest 80% controlling only 7% of the national wealth. So why is this? Why is the top 1% worth more than 50% of all wealth generated? Why are the rich getting richer and everyone else getting poorer? Are the rich smarter than the rest of the world? Are they more talented? What do they know that the rest of the population does not know?

In this book, you are about to uncover some of the answers to these questions. I will start by building a foundation of key things you need to know. Some of these things may seem basic but fully understanding them and the implications they can have on your finances can be life changing. Next, we will review the top obstacles to building wealth. These obstacles, one of which is taxes, are the reasons why many people never achieve real wealth or financial freedom.

We will then outline the key elements of the tax-smart plan, review the goals of the tax-smart plans, and provide a blueprint you can use to build and grow your tax-efficient wealth. Finally, we will walk through the four actionable steps that you can implement starting today to put yourself on the path to building and growing your tax-efficient wealth in the years ahead.

CHAPTER 1

THE FOUNDATION—WHAT YOU NEED TO KNOW

Foundational knowledge is vital in anything you do as it gives you a strong reason and motivation for taking action. Here, we will review a few key basic concepts to help you understand some of the most misunderstood concepts when it comes to taxes and finances. We will spend more time examining taxes for two reasons. First, taxes are your biggest expenses if you make a decent amount of income. Secondly, taxes are complex with all the different rules and tax codes, so most people never attempt to put in the effort to understand some of the basic concepts.

It always amazes me when people say, "Aw, I don't have the time to learn anything about taxes" or "I can't afford to hire a competent Tax Advisor to help me with tax planning and filing of my taxes." These same people get very excited when they get a 1% or 2% annual raise in salaries but don't realize that spending time understanding and planning their taxes can get them 2X,

3X, or even 10X what they're getting in annual raises from their jobs. My goal with this chapter is to get you excited about taxes and other key foundational concepts I will cover here.

Marginal Tax Rates

The Canadian tax system is based on marginal tax rates. This simply means that the more money you make, the more taxes you pay. As your income increases, so does your marginal tax rate. Marginal tax is the dollar amount of tax you pay on any additional dollar of taxable income. Let me illustrate this with a simple example for an individual taxpayer residing in Ontario earning a regular income. In Ontario, below are the 2020 marginal tax rates (Combined Ontario and Federal Tax Rates):

Taxable Income ($)	Marginal Tax Rate (%)
0 to 10,783	0
10,784 to 12,298	5.05
12,299 to 44,740	20.05
44,741 to 48,535	24.15
48,536 to 78,783	29.65
78,784 to 89,482	31.48
89,483 to 92,825	33.89
92,826 to 97,069	37.91
97,070 to 150,000	43.41
150,001 to 150,473	44.97
150,474 to 214,368	47.97
214,369 to 220,000	51.97
220,001 and up	53.53

Based on these rates, if you live in Ontario and earn $50,000 of employment income, you would be in the 29.65% marginal tax bracket and you would pay 29.65% in taxes for every dollar you earn above $48,535. If you earn $100,000 of employment income, you would be in the 43.41% marginal tax bracket, and you would pay 43.41% in taxes for every dollar you earn above $97,070.

Most people often misunderstand marginal tax rates by thinking that your marginal tax rate will be applied to your entire income to determine your total taxes. For example, you may think that if you earn $100,000 in regular income, your taxes payable will be $43,410 because you're in the 43.41% marginal tax rate. This is incorrect, and it is a general misconception. Instead, if you earn $100,000 of income, your taxable income will be $23,848 calculated as:

Taxable Income ($)	Marginal Tax Rate (%)	Calculation	Taxes Payable ($)
0 to 10,783	0		
10,784 to 12,298	5.05	(12,298–10,783) x 5.05%	77
12,299 to 44,740	20.05	(44,740–12,298) x 20.05%	6,505
44,741 to 48,535	24.15	(48,535–44,740) x 24.15%	916
48,536 to 78,783	29.65	(78,783–48,535) x 29.65%	8,969

78,784 to 89,482	31.48	(89,482–78,783) x 31.48%	3,368
89,483 to 92,825	33.89	(92,825–89,482) x 33.89%	1,133
92,826 to 97,069	37.91	(97,069–92,825) x 37.91%	1,609
97,070 to 150,000	43.41	(100,000–97,069) x 43.41%	1,272
Total			**$23,848**

Knowing your marginal tax rate is critical for tax planning and other financial decisions. Without this knowledge, you may end up paying more than your fair share of taxes and keeping less of your income. Remember, wealth accelerates based on how much you can save, not necessarily how much you make in gross earnings. Understanding marginal taxes will play a key role here. In the example above, with adequate planning, it is possible to avoid the additional $1,272 in taxes by keeping your income below $97,070 in the tax year. You could even save more taxes if you plan properly and keep your taxable income below $92,826. Remember, every dollar saved in taxes will help accelerate your wealth. You will see why when we discuss the impact of compound interest shortly.

Different Tax Rates for Different Types of Income

When it comes to taxes, the term "income" isn't quite as straightforward as you might think. In Canada, there are four main distinct groups of income you may have as an individual with a variety of different tax implications. In other words, different types of income attract different tax rates and, in some cases, zero tax! Below are the four main groups of income in Canada:

1. **General income:** This includes income from employment, self-employment, sales commissions, tips and gratuities, pensions and other social benefits, interest, etc.

2. **Dividend income:** This is dividends paid to company shareholders. Dividend income receives a special deduction that can reduce the rate of taxation. However, the effect of the deduction varies.

3. **Capital gains income:** This is the income you make by selling shares or other property, which are taxes on only half the profit made on the sale (except your home, which is exempted from tax when it is your principal residence).

4. **Tax-free income:** This includes income from insurance, income from the sale of your principal residence, gaming and gifts, which are generally tax-free (except gifts from your employer, and

some gifts of capital, such as company shares—if the gift produces income, then the income is usually taxed).

General income sources are taxed the most heavily in Canada. Dividend income and Capital gains income attract lower taxes compared to general income. The best part is that certain income sources are tax-free. In addition to the income sources included in this tax-free income group listed in point 4 above, proceeds from loans such as equity from your home or loan from your tax-exempt insurance policies can also be included in this income group. This fourth group of income represents a great source of tax-free income that can be used to significantly accelerate your wealth.

Depending on the type of income you earn, you may end up keeping less or more of your income. So it is vital to understand this and plan accordingly to structure your income so you can keep more of your money. Again, every dollar saved in taxes will help accelerate your wealth. You will hear this over and over again throughout this book.

Tax Credits vs. Tax Deductions

Before I examine the differences between tax credits and tax deductions, it is important to understand that income tax is based on your taxable income, not your total income. To get to your taxable income, the Income Tax Act allows you to deduct various amounts from your income to arrive at your taxable income. In addition to this, there are many credits that you can use to reduce the taxes payable.

While a few people may be familiar with tax credits and tax deductions, most people don't understand the difference between these two terms. More importantly, I find that taxpayers don't always take advantage of the various tax credits and deductions that are available to reduce their income taxes. As a result, they end up keeping less of their money. So what are the differences between a tax credit and a tax deduction, and why does it matter?

Tax Deductions
Tax deductions reduce your taxable income. They are allowable expenses and adjustments you can claim to reduce your taxable income. This means that if you earned $100,000 in income and had $10,000 in expenses, your taxable income would be $90,000. The tax rates will then be applied to this $90,000 to arrive at your taxes payable. Tax deductions reduce the taxes owed by your marginal tax rate. Examples of allowable deductions include contributions to your Registered Pension Plans (RPP) or Registered Retirement Savings Plan (RRSP), childcare expenses, moving expenses, annual union or professional dues, certain business losses, interest and fees paid for investments, etc.

Tax Credits
While tax deductions reduce your taxable income, tax credits, on the other hand, directly reduce the amount of

taxes due, dollar for dollar. In Canada, tax credits are generally determined by applying a 15% rate to the tax credit amount. In other words, if you have a $1,000 eligible tuition amount, you get a tax credit of $150. There are two types of tax credits:

1. **Nonrefundable tax credits:** These credits help you reduce any taxes you owe and may reduce your tax liability to zero. Examples include personal amounts allowed under the Income Tax Act, charitable donations, and spouse/common-law partner credit.

2. **Refundable tax credits:** These credits also help reduce what you owe on taxes and may also reduce your tax liability to zero. Unlike the nonrefundable tax credits, these credits can result in you actually getting a tax refund if there is any amount left over after reducing your tax to zero. Examples include the goods and services tax/harmonized sales tax (GST/HST) credit and the Working Income Tax Credit.

Tax deductions are generally more valuable if your income is higher since it reduces your tax at your marginal tax rate. If you're in the lowest tax bracket, a deduction and a tax credit are essentially the same since the rate used in calculating the tax credit is approximately the same as the tax rate in the lowest tax bracket. Obviously, if you have the option of choosing between a $1,000 tax deduction and a $1,000 tax credit, the tax credit will be superior as this gives you a dollar-for-dollar reduction in your taxes due compared to the tax deduction that will reduce your taxes due at your marginal tax rate.

It is important you understand all the available tax deductions and tax credits to determine which one applies to you as taxpayers often miss this. Bear in mind that the deductions you are eligible for will change throughout your life. For example, a seventy-year-old taxpayer will be most interested in the age and pension income deductions while a final year university student may only care about tuition deduction. Even though some of these deductions change during your lifetime, many of them apply throughout your life or can be transferred to another taxpayer.

A good practice to adopt before filing your taxes is to obtain a checklist of all allowable deductions and credits and review each one to determine which one you qualify for based on your situation. This small exercise can save you taxes. A dollar saved in taxes can certainly help in accelerating the growth of your wealth.

Tax-Deferred vs. Tax-Free

This is often misunderstood. To be clear, "tax-deferred" _does not_ mean the same thing as "tax-free." Tax-deferred is something that must eventually have taxes paid on it. On the other hand, tax-free will not need any tax payments made.

Tax-Deferred

Tax-deferred accounts allow you to realize immediate tax deductions up to the full amount of your contribution, but future withdrawals from the account will be taxed at your regular income rate. The most common tax-deferred account in Canada is the RRSP. Essentially, with these accounts, taxes on the income are "deferred" to a later date.

This account has its benefits as you get the immediate advantage of paying lower taxes in the current year. Promoters of this plan often encourage high-income earners to max out their tax-deferred accounts to minimize their current tax burdens with the assumption that when they retire, they will likely generate less taxable income and, therefore, find themselves in a lower tax bracket.

Tax-Free

On the other hand, tax-free accounts don't deliver a tax benefit when you contribute to them. Instead, they provide future tax benefits, i.e., returns on the invested funds grow tax-free, and withdrawals at retirement or at a future date are not subject to taxes. In Canada, the most common type of these accounts is the Tax-Free Savings Account (TFSA).

With these accounts, the benefits are realized further in the future as time is needed to grow the funds in the account and to subsequently grow the returns in a tax-free manner. So these accounts are ideal for young adults who have more time to save within this account.

In general, low-income earners are encouraged to focus on funding a tax-free account on the assumption that they are not currently in a high-income tax bracket. Higher-salary earners are encouraged to contribute to a tax-deferred account to get the immediate benefit of lowering their taxable income, which can result in significant value.

While I love both plans and use them as tools for wealth accumulation, careful planning is required when investing in these accounts, particularly, in the tax-deferred account. Remember, our goal is to accelerate our wealth. What that means is that we will likely be in a higher tax bracket in later years as we will likely have more income. As a result, we have to plan accordingly to ensure we don't face a significant tax liability in later years when we withdraw from these accounts.

In addition, if you follow and pay attention to world economic trends, including rising government debt, inflation, etc., you will realize that tax rates are more likely to increase in the future. Having this in mind, we want to be in a position where we withdraw our funds tax-free. I will discuss the strategies we can use to accomplish this in the coming chapters. So keep reading!

The Three Powerful Accelerators

Now that we have examined some of the foundational concepts that will help you save on taxes, let's look at some underlying concepts to help you understand how you can multiply those tax dollars you've saved to quickly accelerate your wealth.

Compound Interest

Compound interest is the principle by which the interest you earn also earns interest, and the interest on that interest earns interest, ad infinitum. This is in contrast to simple interest, where you only earn the same amount of interest each year on your original principal balance. With compound interest, the larger your balance gets, the bigger those interest numbers become. As you may have heard in the past, compound interest is often called the eighth wonder of the world. Compounding is certainly one of the marvels of the universe.

To illustrate the power of compound interest, consider the following question: How much would one penny, doubled every day for one month, equal? If you're like most people, your guess would be around $500. The correct answer? One penny, doubled every day for a month, equals a whopping $10.7 million! This is absolutely shocking to most people, not because the math is too challenging, but, instead, because the answer is so unexpected. We think that a penny is worthless and that one month is a relatively short time. I was in the same boat too as I found this shocking when this same question was posed in a report by Adam Baratta that I read recently.

Compound interest has a similar effect, and just like in the example above, we often underestimate the power of compound interest. If you do the math to solve the question above, you will notice that the exponential growth in the number did not start until day twenty-eight when it skyrocketed. With compound interest, as the numbers get bigger, so does the benefit of compounding. Think of it like a snowflake turning into a giant snowball—the longer the hill is, the bigger the snowball can get.

There is a concept called the "Rule of 72" that helps to simplify the concept of compound interest and its impact. The rule tells us that at a given interest rate, if you divide that rate into seventy-two, the result indicates how many years it will take to double your money when it is compounding. For example, if you earned 8% compound interest, your money would double every nine years (seventy-two divided by eight equals nine); if you earned 10% compound interest, your money would double every 7.2 years. The impact gets even bigger when you compound monthly, weekly, or daily.

Bear in mind that to benefit from the "magic of compounding interest," you need to redeploy that income quickly so that you can also start making returns on the money you made as soon as possible. That is the concept of velocity (to be discussed below).

Some so-called financial gurus or real estate gurus often misunderstand this concept and misapply it when describing the returns from investing in the stock market or real estate. If you earn 10% cash-on-cash return from your real estate investment each year, your investment will not double in 7.2 years if you don't immediately redeploy that return into a similar investment opportunity.

If you invest in the stock markets with the assumptions and uncertainty surrounding investments in many public equity markets, along with exorbitant fees charged by portfolio managers and mutual funds, it is unlikely your investments will double as outlined here. However, it is quite possible to create this "magic of compounding interest" yourself by simply redeploying capital quickly — you just have to have reliable investment sources at your disposal at all times.

As you can see, compound interest can help you accelerate your wealth when applied correctly to the tax dollars you have saved from your tax planning strategies.

Leverage

Some of you would agree that the word "leverage" is more or less a buzz word. Here, leverage simply refers to using other people's money (OPM) — borrowing, incurring debt, taking bank loans, using credit cards, etc.

As you may already know, leverage is a double-edged sword. When poorly used, it can result in an unmanageable debt level that can cause more harm than good. When used judiciously as an investment tool, leverage can be an awesome thing. Without leverage, accumulating wealth will be more challenging — it is not impossible to achieve some level of financial freedom without leverage, but it will take a much longer time and you will never truly achieve significant wealth.

All the billionaires and millionaires achieved wealth by employing some form of leverage in their business, in their personal finance, and in other areas of their endeavors. It is fair to conclude that most of these people accomplished their goal by using real estate because real estate offers a great opportunity to apply this concept of leverage.

The use of leverage maximizes your returns and substantially shortens the time required to attain wealth. For example, if you invest $100,000 in a Guaranteed Investment Certificate (GIC) that has an interest rate of 2% per annum, it would yield a return of $2,000 per year. If you were to take that same $100,000 and use it as leverage to purchase a $500,000 property, assuming the same 2% growth on your new investment value of $500,000, you would get a gross return of $10,000. Which would you prefer?

If you truly understand and embrace this concept of positive leverage, and apply it in your investments over and over again, you will accelerate your wealth accumulation in the same way that compound interest does.

Velocity
This is one concept that most people may be unfamiliar with, particularly when it comes to personal finance. In the world of finance and economics, the velocity of

money is a measurement of the rate at which money is exchanged in an economy. It is the number of times that money moves from one entity to another. In economics, the velocity of money is usually measured as a ratio of gross domestic product (GDP) to a country's money supply.

In Robert Kiyosaki's book *Who Took My Money?* he writes that the velocity of money is one of the reasons why the rich get richer while the average person risks losing a large portion of their savings. According to Robert, as an investor looking to build and accelerate wealth, you'd want to:

1. Invest your money into assets.
2. Get your money back.
3. Keep control of the asset.
4. Move your money into a new asset.
5. Get your money back.
6. Repeat the process.

As you can see, the same money is reinvested into assets over and over again. The term velocity is associated with speed. So how quickly do you want to reinvest? As quickly as possible! There are two important reasons why we should use the velocity of money to our advantage. Firstly, it significantly reduces our risk, and secondly, it allows us to compound income at a faster pace (do you remember the power of compound interest?).

Billionaire Mark Cuban and owner of the NBA's Dallas Mavericks once tweeted: "People create wealth by owning assets that appreciate or create/earn other assets." If you think about this statement, you will see that wealth flows from using your assets to acquire more assets. The underlying force that allows you to do this is the velocity of money.

I hope that, by now, you are beginning to appreciate the extreme power of these three powerful accelerators of wealth—compound interest, leverage, and velocity. Now consider the explosive power of combining all three in your planning!

In the coming chapters, I will show you how you can take the concepts you have learned in this chapter and begin to build a plan to grow and accelerate your wealth. I will show you how to legitimately use available tax breaks to save money that would otherwise have been paid in taxes. Take those dollars and invest in vehicles that will accumulate in a tax-efficient or tax-free manner. Leverage the investments as fast as possible to acquire more assets so that in a few short years, those investments will be earning a lot more than you may be earning at your current job today. Before we get there, let's first talk about the key obstacles that prevent most people from building wealth.

CHAPTER 2

THE OBSTACLES

Truth be told, building wealth is hard. This is why most people never achieve financial freedom. If you search online, you will find millions and millions of books on how to build wealth. You will see the different types of strategies discussed. Some will even say it is easy. They will suggest some simple steps to take to achieve financial freedom and the list goes on and on and on.

So why is it that with the amount of resources available on getting rich, creating wealth, and becoming a millionaire, most people still never achieve financial freedom? The answer is "Obstacles." Obstacles prevent most people from building and growing their wealth. To be clear, there could be millions of obstacles ranging from factors that we can control and those that we cannot control. There is no way I can summarize or tackle all possible obstacles here. Instead, I will focus on four key financial obstacles that often prevent most people from truly building wealth.

Taxes

If you ask most Canadians what their biggest expense is, they will most likely say it's housing costs—mortgage or rent. If you listen to the news media, they are always talking about the top three household expenses:

1. Housing (mortgage or rent)
2. Car payments (loan and interest)
3. Kids' education or childcare (student loans or school fees)

Unfortunately, they are all wrong! According to a recent report from the Fraser Institute, the average Canadian family spent 43.6% of their income on taxes in 2018, more than they spent on housing and other expenses combined. Can you imagine that? This is significant. The average family's total tax bill at 44% is double the amount they're paying on housing costs each year. So if taxes are our biggest expenses, why is it that most people don't pay attention to it? Why is it that most Canadians and the news media get it all wrong? I think there are two main reasons for this.

First, the majority of us are used to withholdings. In other words, we never see this money as our employers take it upfront from our salaries and remit to the government. Second, the amount of other forms of taxes we pay on our everyday purchases seem insignificant on a transaction-by-transaction basis.

The total tax bill considered in the Fraser report reflects taxes families paid to the federal, provincial, and local governments—including income, payroll, sales, property, carbon, health, fuel, and alcohol taxes. Once you begin to put these pieces together, you can now start appreciating the impact of taxes on your personal finances. This is clearly one reason why most people never achieve financial freedom. It is a big obstacle.

To be clear, paying taxes is important for the benefits it provides to our society as a whole. What you have to consider is whether you're paying more than your fair share of taxes. While I highly recommend that you pay whatever taxes you are legally required to pay, you should consider legal options available in our Tax Act to reduce your tax burden.

Nondeductible Interest

The biggest asset we own is our primary residence for those that own their own homes. The cost of buying a home continues to rise, and it is getting increasingly unaffordable for most young people today. As the cost of housing rises, so is our mortgage balance. Added to this is the rising debt of the Canadian household. As a result of all these high mortgage and debt balances, most Canadians are now burdened with high-interest costs associated with these debts. Unfortunately, in Canada, our tax rules generally do not permit a deduction for the mortgage interest related to our primary residence. Furthermore, most interest on other debt we have will also not be deductible, except they are debt incurred directly to earn income from a property or business.

Most of us never put a lot of thought into this as we automatically pay our mortgage each month or every two weeks without examining how much of this payment goes toward the reduction of our principal balance. I encourage you to look at your mortgage statement or your amortization schedule to see the amount of payment that goes toward interest payment alone. You will quickly notice that it is significant.

The fact that you cannot deduct your biggest interest cost is a huge obstacle that will prevent you from growing your wealth. As tax-smart Canadians, one of our goals is to come up with strategies to convert some of these nondeductible interest costs to tax-deductible interest costs.

In certain circumstances, taxpayers can obtain an interest deduction for borrowings made for specific purposes. The general rule of thumb is that interest is deductible to the extent the borrowed monies are used to earn income. However, there are additional accepted circumstances where interest can be deducted for tax purposes based on Canadian jurisprudence and the CRA's administrative positions. With proper planning and advice, taxpayers may be able to structure their borrowings to provide the maximum tax benefit.

Cash Flow Crunch

Have you wondered why you have very little or no money left shortly after your payday? Are you one of those high-income earners that make over $100,000 per annum and still wonder, "Where is all my money?" The clue may be in the diagram below:

Cash flow pattern of the average taxpayer:

INCOME

↓

TAXES

↓

EXPENSES

↓

LITTLE OR NO CASH LEFT TO SAVE OR INVEST

For the average Canadian employee, taxes are taken upfront through payroll withholdings before we see the money. With the funds left, we now have to pay for all our expenses, majority of which are nondeductible for tax purposes, payments like mortgages or rent, car payments, childcare expenses, gas, food, clothing and other household expenses. At the end of the day, we are left with little or no cash to invest. In fact, based on the current trend of rising household debt, a good number of Canadians, unfortunately, will pay for some of these expenses using credit cards, lines of credit, etc. thus, adding additional layers of nondeductible interest costs.

The tax-smart taxpayer will conserve more cash by reverse engineering the cash flow pattern so that there is more cash left over to invest and grow wealth.

Cash flow pattern of the tax-smart Canadian:

INCOME

↓

EXPENSES

↓

TAXES

↓

MORE CASH TO SAVE OR INVEST

By careful tax planning, you can make changes that will allow you to save more of your cash so that at the end of the day, you will have leftover cash you can save and invest to grow and accelerate your wealth. These strategies may include reducing the amount of upfront deductions from your salary, converting some of the after-tax expenses to before-tax expenses, and converting some of your nondeductible interest costs to tax-deductible interest costs, among others.

Inflation

What is inflation? Inflation is the rate at which the general level of prices for goods and services is rising.

I refer to this as the silent killer as we often don't see it. While most Canadians are familiar with inflation, we often underestimate the powerful impact it has on our ability to grow our wealth and eventually achieve financial freedom. Ironically, we often think of financial freedom in terms of dollar value rather than in terms of the purchasing power of our dollars (the amount of goods and services you can buy). At the end of the day, if you're unable to acquire what you need when you need it, then you're not necessarily financially free.

So what's the big deal about inflation, and why should we care?

If you had a $100,000 income five years ago, you could probably afford a decent starter home, take care of your expenses, and have little left to save and invest. Today, if you earn $100,000 income, your purchasing power will be way less. You are likely unable to afford a house today, and even if you can afford one, you will end up incurring debt to keep up with your expenses.

In simple terms, a $100,000 income a year ago with a 5% annual inflation is only worth $95,000 today. And if you consider the fact that the tax rate will increase with time, you can now see why this will quickly become a great obstacle to building sustainable wealth. For those that understand the world economy at a deeper level, you know that inflation will never go away. In fact, the Canadian government and other governments around the world intentionally create inflation with policies. Inflation is needed to deal with the rising debt crisis.

To provide a little bit of insight, the global debt of the world adds up to $255 trillion. This amount is more than three times the world GDP; this ratio is even worse if you look at countries like the United States, Japan, and some European countries. An important question to then consider is: Who is going to pay all of this debt? The reality is that these debts will never be repaid as they've grown to levels that are now unmanageable. As a result, currencies will continue to devalue, allowing this debt to be wiped away via inflation.

Eventually, with this trend, we will get to a point where countries will be forced to go bankrupt, and our dollar will devalue to a point where we only get back pennies on the dollar. To the regular taxpayer, this may seem unlikely, but to the tax-smart Canadian, this is anticipated and will inform decisions on planning strategies to invest wisely and protect wealth.

Now that we have examined the key obstacles, let's dive into the tax-smart plan.

JOIN THE PLAN TO RETIRE WELL MEMBERSHIP

Unfortunately, we have become programmed to do what everyone else is doing. The reason for this is because human psychology lends itself to this herd mentality. There are times when the herd offers protection and other times when following the herd poses a tremendous risk. The tax-smart person understands this dynamic. Risks for the herd become opportunities for those with insight.

Plan to Retire Well is a one-of-a-kind educational platform that has been uniquely designed to offer a course on the fundamentals of successful tax-efficient wealth accumulation. In order to be a successful tax-smart Canadian, we need more information; we need knowledge followed by action. Knowledge combines information about the past and applies it to the ever-changing environments and mindsets of the world. Having keen insights into the dynamic and uncertain future is paramount. However, it is an action that unites every great success. Action is what produces results. Knowledge is only power when it comes into the hands of someone who knows how to take effective action. Ultimate power is the ability to produce the results that you desire most.

Ken Green has helped many of his clients and followers get on the right path to managing their taxes smartly and subsequently growing their wealth.

JOIN OUR MEMBERSHIP PROGRAM
www.plantoretirewell.ca

TAX EFFICIENT WEALTH

+++SPECIAL OFFER+++

$47 monthly subscription, or
$470 one-time annual pay

As a member, you enjoy the following exclusive benefits

- FREE 30-min session with Ken to create a crystal-clear vision for your "Ultimate Personal Financial Success"
- Monthly live calls to discuss tips and strategies, implementation plans, insights from experts, and review the current economic and investment landscape
- Monthly newsletter that is packed with ideas on creating new income sources, investment opportunities, and practical steps to start taking action
- Review of investment opportunities that will allow you to deploy capital immediately (think velocity)
- Rare access to how other members and I are creating new income sources, investing, and accelerating our wealth
- One FREE member-only exclusive dinner party per annum to meet and connect with other members and share ideas
- Access to "Launch Your Side Business in 30 Days from Start to your First Sale" training program and challenge

***CLICK HERE TO
JOIN OUR MEMBERSHIP PROGRAM TODAY***
www.plantoretirewell.ca

CHAPTER 3

THE TAX-SMART PLAN

In this chapter, we will discuss the tax-smart plan. It is a simple plan in direct response to three of the obstacles we discussed in the previous chapter. Before we review the tax-smart plan, let me start by outlining the key goals of the plan:

- Goal # 1—To contribute or save money tax-free
- Goal # 2—To grow or accumulate money tax-free
- Goal # 3—To withdraw or distribute money tax-free

Your wealth can be enhanced dramatically by arranging your affairs, so you can achieve all or some of these goals. If you consider the likelihood that taxes will continue to increase, you will agree with me that it makes so much sense to invest in an environment where you do not have to pay taxes now or sometime in the future. Imagine a situation where you're able to invest with tax-free dollars, allow those investments to grow tax-free, and also withdraw the funds at a future date without paying taxes. If you're able to achieve these goals, you can make your savings grow exponentially. And this is how you accelerate your wealth.

So now, let's examine the plan. The plan is simply to:

1. Eliminate or reduce taxes.
2. Convert nondeductible interest to deductible interest.
3. Increase cash flow.

I will briefly discuss the various ways and strategies we can use to implement these plans. In the next chapter, I will go into a little more detail on the tools we can use to accomplish this.

Eliminate or Reduce Taxes

Reducing taxes or eliminating them, where possible, will certainly help us accomplish our goals here. This is where tax planning plays a critical role. Most people do nothing simply because they've given into the fact that taxes are complex. Rather than doing nothing, you should consider how to turn these tax complexities into tax savings. That's why it is critical to plan.

Planning requires you to ask great questions. How can I sort through the myriad tax credits to find the ones that are right for my situation? What tax deductions can I take to reduce my taxes? What do I need to know before buying a house or making a significant investment? How do I use my RRSP and TFSA to maximize my tax benefits? By asking these questions and working with a qualified tax advisor, you will gain a much better understanding of your tax situation and uncover ways you can save on taxes.

Here are just a few tips and strategies you can consider to save taxes:

- It is important to know your marginal tax bracket and determine if there are deductions you can take or planning ideas to consider to drop to a lower marginal tax bracket. This can save you taxes.
- Carefully review all tax credits to ensure you're taking advantage of those that you are eligible for. Often, tax credits are missed. For example, if you're a first-time homebuyer, you qualify for a one-time nonrefundable federal tax credit of up to $750. If you have a service animal to help cope with an impairment, you can claim the related costs as a medical expense. If you're disabled, you can qualify for a disability tax credit. And starting in 2020, you may be eligible to claim the Canada training credit, a new refundable tax credit, introduced in the 2019 federal budget.
- Take advantage of RRSP and TFSA to reduce or eliminate taxes. Use these tools strategically. For example, if an RRSP will allow you to drop to a lower tax bracket, use it. If you're starting out in life and have not bought your first home yet, consider maxing your RRSP as much as you can so you can use this as part of your down payment for the purchase. Use tax-free cash to

contribute to your TFSA as these investments are not taxed.

- If employment income is your only source of income, consider starting a side business to expand your eligible deductions. If you're considering a side business, it's better to look into a business or freelance opportunity in areas you're passionate to make it less of a job.
- If you're an employee, in addition to your salary, wages and bonuses, you're taxed on the value of the benefits you receive by virtue of your employment. However, certain benefits are tax-free, so it is important to understand these and consider ways you can negotiate with your employer to maximize your benefits.
- If you're an employee receiving stock options from your employer as a benefit of employment, you can develop an "exercise and sell" strategy for the stock options to ensure you consider cash-flow needs, tax consequences, and investment risk. Without careful planning, you will not maximize the tax benefits of your stock options.
- As an employee, consider the benefits of employee deductions permitted under the Canadian Tax Act. Could you negotiate with your employer to structure your work arrangement to allow you to claim certain employee expenses? Could you negotiate the structure of your compensation to include some commission income so you can claim even more deductions?

- If you're self-employed or a small business owner, ensure you take advantage of the Capital Cost Allowance (CCA) claims to reduce your taxes.
- If you own a business and have kids, consider getting them involved in your business and paying them a reasonable wage for the work they do. By doing this, you can income split and save on taxes.
- If you own an unincorporated business, you may generally deduct premiums paid for private health and dental plans, subject to certain conditions and limits. Also, consider the tax benefits of a Health Spending Account (HSA).
- If you're operating a successful unincorporated business, consider whether incorporating would provide additional commercial and tax benefits. The primary tax deferral benefit provided by incorporating can save you a lot of taxes.
- If you have children under eighteen, could you structure your total family income to maximize the benefit from the Canada Child Benefit program? This program provides a tax-free monthly payment to help eligible families with the cost of raising children under eighteen years of age. This benefit is tied to household income. It begins to phase out for adjusted family net income of over $31,120 and is completely phased out for adjusted family income of over $200,000.
- If you have family members, there are a variety of income-splitting techniques you should consider

to lower or eliminate taxes that would otherwise be paid. For example, you can arrange your financial affairs so that the spouse or partner who earns the higher income is paying as much of the family's living expenses as possible, allowing the other person to save and invest. You could gift or loan funds to your spouse or partner so they can make a TFSA contribution. The income earned on these contributions will not be attributed to you while the funds remain in the plan. You could gift money to your children aged eighteen and over to enable them to earn sufficient income to absorb their deductions and credits and to pay for certain expenses that you would ordinarily pay out of after-tax dollars.

- Consider an effective estate plan that can help you minimize tax on and after your death and provide benefits to your surviving family members over the long term. An effective estate plan should provide tax-efficient income during your lifetime, before and after retirement; provide tax-efficient dependent support after your death; provide tax-efficient transfer of your wealth; and protect your assets.

Convert Nondeductible Interest to Deductible Interest

In the previous chapter, we discussed the fact that the huge mortgage payment we make monthly is a huge obstacle to accelerating our wealth. There are two key reasons why this is a huge obstacle. First, it is a cash drain. As you know, without cash, we cannot invest to earn returns, and if we don't have those returns, we cannot deploy them to earn even more returns and thus accelerate our wealth. Second, the interest on the mortgage is not deductible for tax purposes. As a result, we end up paying more and more in taxes.

Given that the mortgage on our home is the largest debt we have that is nondeductible for tax purposes, one of the greatest ways to tackle this obstacle is to convert the nondeductible interest on our home to deductible interest as quickly as possible. We can achieve this by renting out a portion of our home as this will allow us to claim a portion of the interest as a deduction in our tax return. In addition to this, you can obtain a readvanceable mortgage loan and Home Equity Line Of Credit (HELOC) on your principal residence and use this to redeploy the equity in your home for investment purposes. This is sometimes referred to as the Smith Maneuver strategy. To learn more about this concept, you can google and find a book on this written by Fraser Smith.

With this strategy of converting your nondeductible interest to tax-deductible interest, we are employing all three of the powerful accelerators we discussed in Chapter 1—compound interest, leverage, and velocity. As a result, you have the tremendous opportunity to massively accelerate your wealth.

Why is this concept attractive? First, you will pay off your mortgage in half the time. You can accomplish this by taking advantage of the up to 20% mortgage prepayment that most banks allow as well as the principal pay down you get from your monthly or biweekly mortgage payments. However, unlike the regular taxpayer who throws a party to celebrate mortgage freedom, you will be using the otherwise, lazy equity sitting idle and earning no returns to invest in safe and reliable investments earning decent returns.

Second, you will significantly reduce the nondeductible interest you pay on your mortgage. If you look at the interest expense paid on a regular mortgage amortized over twenty years and compare that to the interest paid on a mortgage amortized over ten years, you will realize that your interest cost can reduce by as much as 50%. This is significant. Third, you have access to capital that will allow you create more assets, and by creating more assets that generate returns, you can now deduct the interest cost to optimize taxes. You can now use the additional returns to create even more assets that will continue to generate more and more cash in the years ahead.

Increase Cash Flow

In the previous chapter, we discussed the cash flow crunch faced by the average taxpayer, mostly from the inability to structure their affairs to convert after-tax expenses to before-tax expenses. In addition to this, there is more pressure on the average taxpayer's cash flow as a result of mortgage payment as all the interest costs are significant and nondeductible for tax purposes. As tax-smart investors, we want to create as much cash as possible as this is the only way we can deploy capital to accelerate wealth. Here are some examples to increase your cash flow:

- Look for opportunities to create income, and more importantly, multiple streams of income that will generate cash flow today. Do you have a skill you can deploy as a freelancer? Can you write a book and sell it on eBay? Can you set up an online business that can generate income?
- Review your expenses frequently to look for opportunities to conserve cash. Do you pay for subscriptions that you no longer use? Are you paying for a service you can get at a cheaper rate or even for free? Have you considered using money-saving apps to cut down on your expenses?
- Have you looked at your tax situation for opportunities to convert some of the expenses you currently pay on after-tax basis to before-tax expenses? For example, could you start a business you're passionate about and deduct regular expenses that can qualify as tax-deductible expenses? Could you hire your kids to work for you and convert some of the kids' expenses to tax-deductible expenses?

CHAPTER 4

THE TOOLS

In this chapter, we will discuss the six primary tools we use to accelerate our wealth in a tax-efficient manner. While other tools that can be used, I love these six tools as these are tools we are familiar with and can deploy very easily:

1. Tax-Free Savings Account (TFSA)
2. Registered Retirement Savings Plan (RRSP)
3. Registered Education Savings Plan (RESP)
4. Real Estate (Primary Residence and Rental Properties)
5. Business
6. Tax-Exempt Life Insurance

While the majority are familiar with these tools, few are familiar with the tax benefits provided by these. And even fewer people are familiar with the massive benefits these tools can provide to accelerate your wealth in a tax-efficient way. In this chapter, I will provide a brief description of these tools and the key tax benefits embedded in them. In the next chapter, we will review the powerful blueprint on how you can layer these tools in your tax planning to quickly amplify your wealth. You don't want to miss this, so keep reading.

Tax-Free Savings Account

The TFSA program was introduced in 2009. It is a way for individuals who are eighteen years of age or older and who have a valid social insurance number (SIN) to set money aside tax-free throughout their lifetime. Contributions to a TFSA are not deductible for income tax purposes. However, any amount contributed as well as any income earned in the account (for example, investment income and capital gains) is generally tax-free, even when it is withdrawn. This is the main benefit of the TFSA, the fact that you can withdraw the funds tax-free.

If you borrow to invest in a TFSA, the fees in relation to a TFSA and any interest on money borrowed to contribute to a TFSA are not tax-deductible. The maximum amount that you can contribute to your TFSA is limited by your TFSA contribution room.

You will accumulate TFSA contribution room for each year even if you do not file an Income Tax and Benefit Return or open a TFSA. Below are the contribution rooms for each year since the TFSA was introduced in 2009:

- The annual TFSA dollar limit for the years **2009** to **2012** was **$5,000**.

- The annual TFSA dollar limit for the years **2013** and **2014** was **$5,500**.
- The annual TFSA dollar limit for the year **2015** was **$10,000**.
- The annual TFSA dollar limit for the years **2016** and **2018** was **$5,500**.
- The annual TFSA dollar limit for the year **2019** is **$6,000**.
- The TFSA annual room limit will be indexed to inflation and rounded to the nearest $500.

So if you have never contributed to your TFSA account and you were at least eighteen years old in 2009, you will have a total contribution room of **$63,500** as of 2019. Investment income earned by and changes in the value of your TFSA investments will not affect your TFSA contribution room for current or future years. All TFSA contributions made during the year, including the replacement or recontribution of withdrawals made from a TFSA, will count against your contribution room.

At any time in the year, if you contribute more than your allowable TFSA contribution room, you will be considered to be overcontributing to your TFSA, and for each month that the excess amount remains in your account, you will be subjected to a tax equal to 1% of the highest excess TFSA amount in the month.

You can give your spouse or common-law partner money to contribute to their TFSA without having that amount, or any earnings from that amount being attributed back to you, but the total contributions you each make to your own TFSAs cannot be more than your TFSA contribution room.

Registered Retirement Savings Plan

An RRSP is a retirement account that was established by the Government of Canada in 1957. RRSPs were introduced by the government to help Canadians save for retirement. The main benefit of RRSPs is that tax on RRSP contributions is deferred until retirement. In other words, any income you earn in the RRSP is usually exempted from tax as long as the funds remain in the plan; you generally have to pay tax when you receive payments from the plan.

Because RRSPs are registered accounts, they're subject to certain rules. One of the most important rules concerns the amount of money you can contribute to the account in any given year; it's either 18% of your past year's income or a maximum amount, whichever is smaller. The maximum amount is determined each year. For example, in 2019, the maximum amount was $26,500, and in 2020, the maximum amount is $27,230. Any unused contribution room can be carried forward to the next year.

Any income you earn in the RRSP is usually exempted from tax as long as the funds remain in the plan. However, you generally have to pay tax when you cash in, make withdrawals, or receive payments from the plan. When you withdraw funds from an RRSP, your financial institution withholds the tax. The rates depend on your residency and the amount you withdraw. For residents of Canada, the rates are:

- 10% (5% in Quebec) on amounts up to $5,000
- 20% (10% in Quebec) on amounts over $5,000 up to including $15,000
- 30% (15% in Quebec) on amounts over $15,000

Note that the tax that was withheld may not always be enough to account for the tax you owe at your tax bracket. You may have to pay more tax on the withdrawal when you include the withdrawal on your Income Tax and Benefit Return for that year.

There are two exceptions that allow you to withdraw from your RRSP for purposes other than retirement. However, you will need to repay the amount:

- Home Buyers' Plan – You can withdraw up to $35,000 for a down payment on your first home and repay over fifteen years.
- Lifelong Learning Plan – You can withdraw up to $10,000 per year to a maximum of $20,000 for school and repay over ten years.

The TFSA and RRSP are the two most popular registered accounts in Canada, and below, I have provided a table to summarize and compare the pros and cons of these accounts to help provide better clarity to you:

Comparison of TFSA vs. RRSP		
Criteria	**TFSA**	**RRSP**
Flexibility of Account	Can be withdrawn anytime and used for anything	Withdrawal will result in the payment of taxes except in situations where you're buying your first home or under the Lifelong Learning Plan
Investment options	You can choose your own investments	You can choose your own investments
Tax rules	Tax-sheltered growth on investments	Tax-sheltered growth on investments
Direct Contributions	Can contribute directly based on your contribution room	Can contribute directly based on your contribution room
Tax deductions	No tax deduction on contribution	You can claim a tax deduction in the year you make a contribution
Withdrawal	Withdraw any amount at any time, without paying income taxes. You can also replace the amount of the withdrawal in the same year if you have available TFSA	Withdraw any amount at any time, subject to income taxes. You lose the contribution room for any amount withdrawn

	contribution room	
Contribution limits	Annual maximum varies each year. In 2020, maximum contribution is $6,000	Annual maximum varies each year. In 2020, it is 18% of previous year's earned income or $27,230, whichever is lower
Expiration	No expiry	RRSPs must be converted to a Registered Retirement Income Fund (RRIF) by December 31 of the year you turn seventy-one

Registered Education Savings Plan

An RESP is a special savings account for parents who want to save for their child's education after high school. It is a tax-advantaged account where funds can be invested in countless ways similar to the investments in an RRSP or TFSA. With an RESP account, there is no tax deduction for the contributor for amounts contributed to the plan. Any Canadian (usually parents, grandparents, and other family members) can open an RESP account on behalf of a child (the beneficiary).

The contributions and the income from the plan are generally paid to the beneficiaries. Income earned on the contributions in the plan is paid to the beneficiaries as educational assistance payments (EAPs). If the contributions are not paid out to the beneficiary, the promoter usually pays them to the subscriber at the end of the contract. Subscribers do not have to include the contributions in their income when they get them back.

On receipt of payment from the promoters of the plan, the beneficiaries have to include the EAPs in their income for the year in which they receive them. However, they do not have to include the contributions they receive in their income.

There are three main benefits of the plan. First, you save on taxes. While there are no tax deductions from the contributions made, there are no income or capital gains taxes as long as the money remains invested in the account. Once it is withdrawn and used for an approved education expense, which can include tuition, housing, books, or even living expenses while in school, investment gains will be subject to taxes in the hands of the students. Given that students typically have little or no income, it is likely that no taxes will be paid on this income.

Second, contributions to the RESP are matched by the government. In 1998, the government introduced the Canada Education Savings Grant (CESG), a program that promised to match 20% of any RESP contributions up to $2,500 per account, per child, per year (i.e., a maximum government grant of $500 per child). Third, there is flexibility in how the funds in the account can be invested to help diversify risks and returns. Options for investments include mutual funds, ETFs, GISs, stocks, bonds, and a number of other alternative investments.

Although an RESP is a great tool for saving taxes and preparing for your kid's education, there are some limitations. The maximum contribution to an individual RESP is $50,000 and the total CESG any child can receive is $7,200. In addition, if a child decides not to study after high school, and there are no siblings to transfer the funds to, the funds may be transferred to the contributor's persona RRSP on a tax-free basis. However, all government CESG grants must be repaid as soon as an RESP is closed.

Real Estate (Primary Residence and Rental Properties)

Real estate is probably the best tax-advantaged asset class you will find. It is one of our primary tools for growing and accelerating our tax-efficient wealth. In Canada, we pay no capital gains taxes on the sale of our primary residence. This is a huge tax break. In addition to this, there are several other tax advantages of owning rental real estate.

First, you can claim deductions on certain expenses directly related to the operation of the rental real estate. So long as your primary aim is to generate income from the property, you can deduct all reasonable expenses incurred to generate rental income. These expenses may include property taxes, insurance, mortgage interest, repairs, advertising, legal and professional fees, office space, including home office, business equipment, etc.

Second, you can depreciate the cost of the property. If you own a property used for business or rental for a year or more, the government allows you to depreciate the cost of the property over time. In Canada, it is called CCA. With the use of the CCA, you can deduct the property's loss in value over its expected useful life, generally 25 years. The CCA provides a huge tax advantage for owners of rental real estate.

Third, when you sell real estate for more than you originally purchased it for, the profit will be taxed as capital gains, which is typically a lower tax rate than ordinary income tax. Fourth, if you own real estate that is used primarily for earning income from a business, you may defer and roll capital gains into replacement properties under section 44 or 44.1 of the Canadian Income Tax Act.

Finally, real estate also provides the opportunity to leverage. As I discussed in Chapter 1, the power of leverage is one of the accelerators of wealth, and this is one thing real estate offers. The fact that you can pull out equity without tax consequences and leverage that to create new assets makes real estate one of the best tools for building and accelerating wealth.

Business

Owning and operating a business is certainly one of my favorite tools for managing taxes and accelerating wealth. Not only does a business give you great flexibility for the deduction of expenses, it also creates a valuable asset that continues to generate cash flow today and in the future. In addition to this, you enjoy all the other benefits that come with owning a business such as your ability to control your own destiny, the flexibility to choose whom to work with, the opportunity to pursue your passion, and the pride in building something of your own, among other benefits.

If you take a look at most economies in the world, Canada included, small businesses account for the majority of the jobs created. In other words, small businesses are the engines of most of these economies. In Canada and in most of the developed economies, the government recognizes this, and as a result, there are associated tax benefits in the Tax Act to encourage new businesses so that these businesses can continue to create jobs for the economy.

Some of these benefits include the preferential tax rates that businesses enjoy. For example, if you own a business in Ontario that qualifies as a Canadian Controlled Private Corporation (CCPC), your combined tax rate up to a business limit of $500,000 is only 12.2% compared to the top marginal personal tax rate of 53.53% on income in excess of $220,001.

We certainly use business as a key tool in reducing and eliminating taxes so we can accumulate more cash for growing and accelerating our wealth. It is an effective strategy for converting what would otherwise be an after-tax expense to a tax-deductible expense. It is also a smart way to split income among family members, which effectively reduces or eliminates taxes that would otherwise be paid.

Expenses such as vehicle expenses, meals and entertainment, travel and home business expenses that the normal person pays with after-tax dollars can be strategically converted to before-tax expenses. In the coming chapters, as we look at the blueprint and implementation strategies, you will get a better understanding and appreciation of the power of using business as a tool for tax planning and wealth accumulation.

Tax-Exempt Life Insurance

Of the four tax-free options that our tax law permits, the use of tax-exempt life insurance is one of the less known tax strategies. You're likely familiar with the other three options, some of which I have discussed here already—Principal Residence, TFSA, and Lottery Winnings.

Under section 143(3) of the federal Income Tax Act, assets accumulate within a tax-exempt life insurance contract are free of annual accrual taxation. When you pass away, any proceeds of the policy are distributed to your beneficiaries on a tax-free basis outside the scope of your estate, bypassing its associated costs. In light of our tax planning to build and accelerate tax-efficient wealth, tax-exempt insurance is a no-brainer tool that allows for:

- Tax-deferred growth, similar to the registered pool of capital in an RRSP
- Potential for tax-free income during retirement
- Tax-free distribution upon your death

Below is a quote from the CA Magazine (now PIVOT Magazine) published by the Chartered Professional Accountants of Canada (previously known as the Canadian Institute of Chartered Accountants):

"Life insurance is still an excellent investment tool... one of the few investments that allow for the tax-sheltered accumulation of funds and at the same time covers the risk of death. ***The pretax compounding effect and the tax-free access to this accumulating fund are two of the attractions of life insurance***. The tax-free maturity on death is the ultimate plus."

Let me draw your attention to the italicized and bolded text (italic and bold are all mine) because I think this is one of the most understood and understated benefits of tax-exempt life insurance. Tax-exempt life insurance is the only product that allows you to double-dip your investments. In other words, by investing in a tax-exempt life insurance policy, you have the opportunity to earn a guaranteed rate of return that compounds year after year. At the same time, you can withdraw up to 100% of the invested funds and invest the proceeds in another investment vehicle to earn additional returns without any impact on the original guaranteed returns from the insurance policy.

Essentially, you could invest the SAME money in two different places at the same time!

So why is the use of tax-exempt life insurance not as common given the tremendous tax advantages it provides and the fact that you can double-dip? There may be a few reasons:

1. **Lack of Knowledge:** This is probably one of the biggest reasons why people don't consider life insurance as a tax planning tool or even as a tool to protect the financial welfare of their loved ones. There is so much misinformation about insurance, and in the midst of this kind of information, it's challenging for most to see the real benefits of having insurance as a great financial and tax planning tool.
2. **Insurance is expensive:** Truth be told, insurance is expensive, particularly, the kind of life insurance (whole life and universal life) that is suitable for tax planning purposes. With the evergrowing costs of keeping up and managing family budgets to pay for things like food, clothing, housing, daycare, car payments, kids' education, etc., insurance is just outside of those "necessities" when money is tight.

3. **Insurance provided through your job:** Many people are offered life insurance as part of their employee benefits package and often decide not to get additional insurance. They forget that coverage provided by this kind of employer-provided insurance is often not sufficient. In addition, if you leave the job, it's typically the type of insurance that doesn't "move on" with you.
4. **Life insurance—it's on my list...eventually:** There's no deadline on life insurance, no mandate from the government on purchasing it. Your parents may have never talked to you about its importance, and it's certainly not the most invigorating topic for conversation. As a result, most never get to it.

CHAPTER 5

THE BLUEPRINT

How do we use and layer the tools discussed in the previous chapter to massively accelerate our wealth? This is what the average taxpayer is unfamiliar with. We have all these tools at our disposal, but we don't make the connections to figure out how we can use these to significantly cut down on our taxes. We don't take advantage of these tools to rapidly accelerate our wealth.

In this chapter, I will discuss the exact step-by-step process for layering the tools I discussed in the previous chapters to build and massively accelerate your wealth. This is where the magic happens. You can use this blueprint as the basis of your implementation plan to achieve your goals of accelerating your wealth as fast as possible. The blueprint is broken down into the following five stages:

Stage 1 — Save Tax Efficiently
Stage 2 — Invest/Leverage/Grow Tax Efficiently
Stage 3 — Invest/Leverage/Grow Tax Efficiently with Velocity

Stage 4—Invest/Leverage/Grow Tax Efficiently with 10X Velocity

Stage 5—Withdraw Tax-Free

Now, let me provide a brief overview of each of these stages below:

Stage 1—Save Tax Efficiently

This is the building stage where we're saving and putting money away in a tax-efficient and tax-free manner. If you recall, one of the goals of our tax-smart plan we discussed in Chapter 3 is to save tax-free. So, at this stage, you certainly want to use all the tools at your disposal to accumulate funds in a tax-free basis by first using your RRSP and then, other tax-efficient tools. See the illustration below for the depiction of the blueprint for this stage.

The amount of savings you allocate to each of these tools will depend on your situation. If you are in your twenties and thirties, my suggestion is to contribute the majority of your savings to your RRSP and some to your TFSA for your emergency account. Obviously, the amount you contribute to your RRSP will depend on other credits you may have to offset your taxes, such as tuition credit, charitable contributions, etc. Consider taking full advantage of these credits first so you can allocate more funds to your TFSA as opposed to your RRSP. Also, you'd want to buy a tax-exempt insurance policy at this stage and plan to fund for eight, ten, or

TAX EFFICIENT WEALTH

twenty years. If you can afford it, it is critical to get as much insurance coverage as you can as you have time on your side and your rates will be much lower. If you can't afford it, then buy a term insurance that can be converted in the future to a tax-exempt life insurance.

If you're in your forties and fifties, the allocation of savings will depend on your income level and how much you already have in your RRSP portfolio. If you are in the high-income bracket, and you have not consistently contributed to your RRSPs over the years, you should consider contributing as much as you can to the RRSP to offset your tax liability. If on the other hand, you have a huge RRSP portfolio, you'd want to pay more attention to maximizing your TFSA contributions as well as other non-registered accounts. At this stage, you should certainly have a tax-exempt life insurance policy that you fund aggressively using tax-free funds from your TFSA and tax refund.

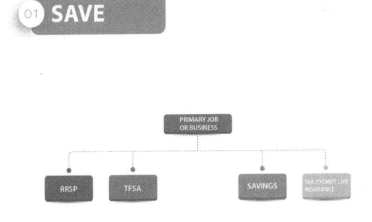

Stage 2—Invest/Leverage/Grow Tax Efficiently

At this stage, you'd want to start investing and using leverage to accelerate your investments. Here are a few things you should consider doing at this stage:

- Continue to aggressively fund your RRSP, TFSA, Tax-Exempt Life Insurance and other savings vehicles you have. Where possible, use tax-free or tax-efficient funds to fund your TFSA and Tax-Exempt Life Insurance.
- If you are a salaried employee with T4 as your only source of income, start a side hustle in what I refer to as your "passion" business. Essentially, this is any business you would love to do for the rest of your life. In other words, when people see you working your side hustle, they can't tell whether you're working or playing. You want a side hustle that is an extension of your lifestyle. For example, I love the game of chess and I have created a side hustle around the game of chess to fulfill my passion. My only caution here is that if you intend to transition from your full-time job to your "passion" business as your new full-time gig, then you have to make sure you have a "passion" business that has a potential to be profitable. By starting and running a "passion" business, you can start shifting some of your regular after-tax expenses to before-tax expenses. At the same time, you may also have the ability to shift income to optimize your tax situation.

- Start building a family at this stage if you don't already have one. If you run a business, get your family members involved in the business. This can be a great tool to teach young kids about money, business, and life. It also presents a great opportunity to income slip among family members. Keep excess funds in the corporation and invest these within the corporation.
- If you don't have a principal residence, this is the time to buy your first principal residence. If you're in your twenties and thirties, you should consider moving at least two to three times before you settle in your dream home in order to take advantage of the principal residence exemption in our tax law. These moves have to be done strategically to ensure the tax-free capital is immediately redeployed in the acquisition of new assets. To buy your first principal residence, use funds from your RRSP and TFSA for your down payment. If you have a corporation, you can also borrow from your corporation to fund your down payment. Rent part of your home to generate rental income and increase your savings rate.
- Get into real estate as soon as possible. I know we live in a time where housing is not cheap, particularly if you live in the Greater Toronto Area. However, this should not be an excuse to not get into real estate. There is no better time than now! Use your creativity and figure out ways you can make it happen. I've bought real estate multiple times without using my own money, and

I know many people that have done the same, even during these times.

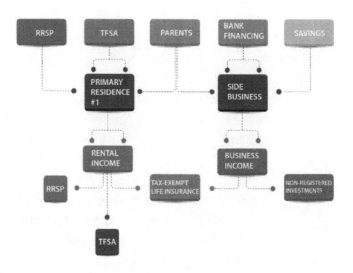

Stage 3—Invest/Leverage/Grow Tax Efficiently with Velocity

At this stage, we will continue to double down on our savings just as we did in stages 1 and 2. Now, we have to start thinking about the velocity of money. Here are a few things to consider at this stage:

- Approximately three to five years after buying your first principal residence, you should buy your first rental property. You will notice that your buying experience will be easier than your experience the first time you bought your primary residence. And it will only get better from here as you buy more and more real estate. Sources of funds for this purchase can come from your tax-exempt life insurance, TFSA, savings, and home equity.
- In another two to three years after buying your first rental property, it will be time to buy a new principal residence and move. Depending on how much equity you have in the home and how well you've managed your savings and investments, you may be able to move to your new primary residence and keep your existing home as a rental. If you don't have the financing to support this, you can sell your first primary residence. Note that the purpose of moving to a second primary residence is not necessarily to move to a bigger house that you don't really need but to leverage the fact that you don't have to pay taxes on the sale or change in the use of your first primary residence.
- You should also start accelerating your savings rate and investments at this stage. You should be using funds from your equity and tax-exempt life insurance to invest in safe vehicles and ventures in non-registered accounts, mortgages, and businesses, etc.

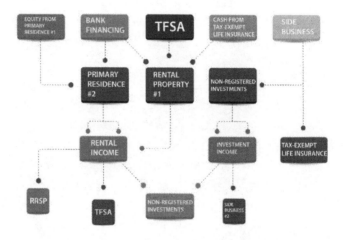

Stage 4—Invest/Leverage/Grow Tax Efficiently with 10X Velocity

At this stage, you will experience velocity at its full force as the growth in your asset will potentially accelerate. Here are some things to consider at this stage:

- You can leverage the three real estate properties you have in stage 3 to buy three new properties, one of which will be your third primary residence. Depending on the amount of savings you've accumulated in your accounts including the cash

reserve in your tax-exempt life insurance, you may be able to acquire an additional rental property here.
- If done properly, you will likely have about six to eight properties at this point, all generating rental income including your primary residence as you will continue to rent part of your home. This process should take you anywhere from seven to fifteen years. If you repeat the process for another ten to fifteen years, you will have more than 10X your wealth.
- At this stage, you want to set up a charitable foundation to fund causes important to you. Consider using life insurance to fund the charity in order to multiply the charitable impact of the causes important to you in your lifetime and for generations to come. This is how you create your own legacy.

TAX EFFICIENT WEALTH

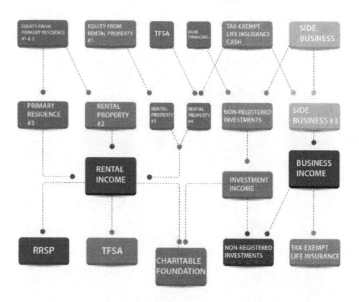

Stage 5—Withdraw Tax-Free

This is what I refer to as the "Tax-Free Zone." At this stage, you will continue to invest. However, you don't have to keep working at the nine-to-five job you hate. You can now work in the business you love and do the meaningful work that gives your life meaning and purpose. You now have the freedom to give more to your charitable causes, to your kids and grandkids. You can live a tax-free life if you so desire as you will only withdraw funds on a tax-free basis. If planned carefully, you can withdraw funds from your RRSP and pay little or no tax. You can also plan accordingly to benefit from government programs like the Canada Pension Plan (CPP), Old Age Security (OAS), and Guaranteed Income Supplement (GIS).

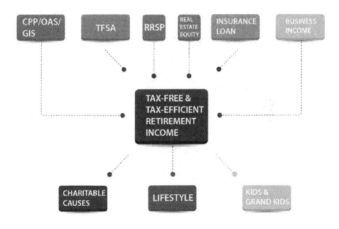

CHAPTER 6

THE IMPLEMENTATION

Nothing happens without implementation. So, in this chapter, we will discuss how you can take what you have learned and put it to work. My heart will be broken if you read this entire book and say to yourself, "This is an excellent book! I've learned so much from this book," and then do nothing to implement the ideas you've learned to help improve your financial position.

For this reason, this is the most important chapter!

The implementation plan is broken down into the following four actionable steps:

Action Step 1—Vision
Action Step 2—Belief
Action Step 3—Assess
Action Step 4—Execute

Action Step 1 — Vision

The first step is to start with the end in mind by casting a very clear vision of what you want in life. This vision will drive the goals you want to accomplish in life. Once you're clear on your vision and goals, you will now develop a plan to document the road map to help you achieve your dreams.

Casting a clear vision begins with your dreams for the future. Dreams have power and they help increase your imagination by allowing you to see possibility in your life beyond your current circumstances. Albert Einstein once said:

"Imagination is more important than knowledge. For knowledge is limited to all we now know and understand, while imagination embraces the entire world, and all there ever will be to know and understand."

When you dream, you think creatively about the life you would love to live. Next, we turn the dreams into a vivid vision by putting this on a vision board. By doing this, we turn the thoughts and dreams in our head into something real and tangible that we can see.

Once we have our vision, we will develop our goals to help us accomplish our dreams. In developing our goals, we have to make the goals *SMARTER* goals and support them with key motivations. The key motivations keep you emotionally connected to your goals. They provide the answer to why the goal is important, to what is at stake, and why you're passionate about accomplishing your goals.

Attributes of a SMARTER Goal

S—Specific: Smarter goals are specific. They are not vague or general. They are very, very specific. For example, if I have a goal to write a book, I can make this more specific by saying my goal is to write a book titled "My life in the tax lane." This is very specific as it is focused on a specific book.

M—Measurable: Smarter goals must be quantified. A goal to lose weight is not measurable. However, a goal to lose 35 pounds is measurable because you can measure this.

A—Actionable: Smarter goals are actionable. This means you want to start them with a good action verb like, *write*, *finish*, or *eliminate*. For example, a goal *to write two blog posts a week* is a lot more actionable than a goal *to be more consistent in blogging*.

R—Realistic: Smarter goals are realistic. In other words, they are not unrealistic. While the goals should be outside of your comfort zone, they should not be so far outside of your comfort zone that it's unrealistic. These goals should challenge you and make you feel a little bit of fear, uncertainty, and doubt.

T—Time-bound: Smarter goals must have a deadline. This creates a sense of urgency, gives you focus, and ensures you're going to achieve your goal. For example, a goal to lose 20 pounds by April 1, 2021 is much stronger than a goal to lose 20 pounds.

E—Exciting: Smarter goals have to be personally compelling. You have to get excited about your goals. If your goals are not compelling, you will likely quit when you hit roadblocks along the way.

R—Relevant: Smarter goals must be relevant. This means they must be appropriate for the season you're in. For example, if you're in a new career, a goal to take thirty days off may not be appropriate for you.

To complete this step, here are the suggested action steps you can take:

- Start by dreaming. Grab a pen and start writing down your dreams. Don't filter. Don't hold back. Just write. As you dream, it may be helpful to ask yourself these questions:

    o What future do you see for yourself?
    o Where would you live?
    o Where would you work?
    o What type of work will you be doing?
    o What would you be doing?
    o If you run a business, what kind of clients would you work with?
    o What brings you joy and fulfillment?

- o What contributions would you make to the society?
- o What legacy would you leave?

- Once you finish your dreams, and you have a clear vision of what you want, put it all on a vision board where you will see it daily. Represent your dreams with pictures where possible. If you have a vision of living on a beach house, get a picture of the beach house you want and put it on the vision board.
- Where possible, go experience some of your dreams. For example, if you want to live in a beach house, take a tour of a beach house and experience for yourself what it feels like to be in a beach house. If your vision is to drive a Ferrari, go to a Ferrari dealership and take a test drive. Experiencing your dreams like this brings your vision alive and drives a stronger motivation to accomplish your dreams.
- The final step here is to start breaking down your vision into concrete goals using the SMARTER goal framework discussed above.

Once you've developed your goals, they should be written down — short term and long term. By taking just a few minutes each morning to look at your vision and read your long-term goals, you will put your day into perspective. You will think about them every day. If you think about them every day and spend your days working toward them, they'll manifest.

Remember this, achieving goals is science. There's no confusion or ambiguity to it. If you follow a simple pattern, you can accomplish all of your life goals, no matter how big they are. It starts with having a vivid picture of your long-term goals, writing them down, and reviewing them every single day.

Action Step 2—Belief

To be successful at anything in life, you must have the right mindset and belief system. You must believe in the possibility! When it comes to building wealth, we have to change our mindset around money and our belief system.

Money Mindset
A money mindset is your unique and individual set of core beliefs about money and how money works in the world. It is your overriding attitude about money. It shapes what you believe you can and cannot do with money, how much money you believe you're allowed, entitled, and able to earn, how much you can and should spend, the way you utilize debt, how much money you give away, and your ability to invest with confidence and success.

Given the potential powerful impact your money mindset has on your relationship with money, it is important to understand your money mindset. Understanding your money mindset and where it came from helps you change it. It is important to pay attention to your thoughts, behaviors, and actions around money. Your thoughts about money will influence your feelings. And your feelings will affect your behavior.

When it comes to money mindset, there are two extremes—Scarcity/Lack and Wealth/Abundance. Most of us will fall in between these two extremes. If you think money is a scarce commodity, you'll feel stressed and anxious. You won't be generous. On the other hand, if you think that there is sufficient money to go around, you'll feel calm, positive, and optimistic. You'll openly share and be more generous.

One suggested approach for uncovering your money mindset is to test yourself by marking True or False to the following statements:

- I'm not good with money.
- I always make the wrong money decisions.
- I'm financially learning disabled.
- I'm not good with numbers.
- Money can't buy you love.
- Money makes the world go around.
- Rich people are snobby and shallow.
- Poor people are hardworking and noble.
- There's a limited supply of money in the world.

This exercise along with many other ideas can help increase your awareness of your money mindset. In addition to this, you can create more awareness by noticing how you behave from time to time. For instance, when you go out for coffee with a friend, do you pick up the bill, or do you not pick up the bill?

Belief System

As you become more aware of your mindset, you'll encounter your own limiting beliefs and money blocks that get in the way of change. When it comes to making a lasting change, limiting beliefs are the only things holding you back. While it is normal to have these beliefs, you have to work continually to uncover these beliefs and money blocks, dissolve them, and release them so you can build a healthier and more confident relationship with your wealth.

Some of the actions you can take here may include rewriting your limiting beliefs as positive money affirmations. For example, if you have a belief that says "I don't know how to deal with money because my family is not good at managing it." You can rewrite this as your new reality as follows: "I have now increased my knowledge of money, and I am a successful money manager who has transformed the old family history of money mismanagement. I am using my resources to take good care of myself and my family and to do good in the world."

A few final thoughts on money mindset and belief systems:

- Remember, money is only a tool, so it is important to consider it as such. While money

can solve a lot of problems, it will not make you happier or give you a more fulfilled life.
- Develop a money mindset that keeps you in control. You want to have control over money, and don't let money control you. If you're controlled by money, you will be desperate. If you're desperate, you will cheat, steal, do stupid things, end up in jail, and eventually lose all your money. Money is not attracted to desperate people. I love this quote by Edmund Burke:

"If we command our wealth, we shall be free; if our wealth commands us, we are poor indeed."

- Understand that character is way superior to money. If you are a jerk when you're broke, you will be a bigger jerk when you're rich. Money will not necessarily change who you are; it will only augment who you are.
- Money will not make a significant difference in how you and I live. This quote by Benjamin Graham sums it up nicely:

"Money isn't making that much difference in how you and I live. We're both going down to the cafeteria for lunch and working every day and having a good time. So don't worry about money, because it won't make much difference in how you live."

Action Step 3—Assess

Now that you know what your future looks like, at this stage, you will have to assess and evaluate your current situation to determine what your reality looks like. You will do this by looking at your income statement, balance sheet, talent/skill level, relationships, and age.

Income Statement
One of the greatest mistakes I made early on in life and one that I see most people make today on the path to financial freedom is the lack of a strong focus on what I refer to as the "GAP." The math equation below illustrates what the "GAP" is:

Income – expenses – taxes = GAP

For many years, I was obsessed with growing my earned income and paid little attention to the "GAP" or anything else for that matter in the equation above. Today, household debt is going through the roof because most people have paid little or no attention to the "GAP." It is one of the leading causes of high-profile bankruptcies — both in our personal lives and in our businesses.

To achieve financial freedom and set yourself up for building and accelerating your wealth, you have to be obsessed with the "GAP." If you do this, you will automatically pay attention to all the variables that make up the "GAP" — your income, your expenses, and your taxes.

From my personal experience and from what I have seen over the years working with many clients, you will struggle financially if you don't focus on maintaining a positive "GAP." And to accelerate your wealth in a tax-efficient manner, you will have to focus on aggressively growing your "GAP." There are so many ways to accomplish this. Here are two practical ideas to consider:

1. **Start with the easy wins:** While all the variables in the equation are important, the easiest place to start is with your expenses since this can give you immediate results and momentum. I recognize it can be challenging to make changes to our everyday lives and cut out certain expenses as we're often reluctant to do this. What I find that works is to surround yourself with others that can hold you accountable. Also, you can consider taking an extreme approach and cut out everything. By doing this, you will often discover things you don't miss. For the things you really miss, you can bring them back in and figure out ways to pay less for them.

2. **Use your assets:** Often, we complain that we have no money or no income, but we're surrounded by assets that are lying idle. Assets ranging from our knowledge and experiences to the things we own lying around our homes and the equity sitting idle in our big homes. You need to be creative in ways you can use the assets you have to generate more income that will help you increase your "GAP." Consider the various ways

you can earn additional income doing what you love ranging from starting an online business to coaching, teaching, and providing great information that others may need.

The path to a strong financial well-being is simply solving this math equation. Solving the math equation will require you to know all the variables that go into this equation. If you can manage the variables, you can certainly manage your "GAP."

Balance Sheet
When you look at your balance sheet, you're primarily focusing on your net worth. It is important to assess your net worth as wealth is ultimately measured in terms of net worth.

Your net worth is the amount by which your assets exceed your liabilities. In simple terms, net worth is the difference between what you *own* and what you *owe*. If your assets exceed your liabilities, you have a positive net worth. Conversely, if your liabilities are greater than your assets, you have a negative net worth.

Net Worth = Assets − Liabilities

If your net worth is negative, it means you owe more than you own. If it is positive, you own more than you owe. Negative net worth does not necessarily indicate that you are financially irresponsible; it just means that—right now—you have more liabilities than assets.

Since net worth is the primary measure of wealth, we'd want to assess our net worth on a regular basis and determine changes we can make to accelerate our net worth. As part of this assessment, you have to pay very close attention to things that can accelerate your net worth. There are basically two ways to increase your net worth:

1. **Acquire assets:** As you buy more assets, you increase your net worth. However, to accelerate your net worth, you just don't acquire any assets; you have to focus on acquiring assets that have the potential to skyrocket in value over time. You focus on assets that have the potential to generate more assets. For example, buying a fancy car will increase your assets (a new car that has value). However, at the same time, buying a car will also deplete another class of assets (the cash used to purchase the car) or increase your liability (if you buy the car using debt). Over time, the value of the car will reduce, which will result in lower net worth. On the other hand, if you purchase an asset like real estate rental, the value of the real estate will increase over time. In addition, real estate rental has the potential to generate cash, which will increase the value of your asset. So you'd want to pay very close attention to the types of assets you acquire.

2. **Pay down debt:** Paying down debt will increase your net worth, and acquiring new debt will reduce your overall net worth. When we assess our debts, we have to pay attention to the type of debt. Ideally, you only want to incur debt to acquire assets that have the potential to increase your overall net worth and add new assets to your balance sheet. So if you want to pay down debt, focus on consumer debt and all other debt that are not directly used to purchase productive assets. Often times, these types of debts result in interest costs that are not deductible for tax purposes.

Talents/Skills

To create wealth, you must assess yourself and determine your talent and what skills you may need to upgrade. You have to develop a mindset that living is a lifelong learning experience. As a result, you must regularly invest in yourself. If you don't do it, no one else will.

You will certainly live a mediocre life if you don't constantly invest in yourself. If you want to live a fruitful life, read and learn from those that are living a fruitful life and model what they do. If you want to be promoted to earn more income, hang out with those that have been promoted and learn from them. If you want to achieve financial success, model those that have achieved financial success.

You must be intentional to grow into the life you want by constantly reading, listening to podcasts, and actively implementing the things you learn to grow and get the results you want in life.

It is suggested that if you invest 10% of your income on yourself, you will yield a 100X or more return on that investment. For every dollar you spend on your education, skills, and relationships, you'll get at least hundred dollars back in returns. While I don't have any facts to back this up, I will agree with this. There is something truly powerful about knowledge, particularly knowledge that is put into use via taking action to implement what you've learned.

A key component of personal growth is to get coaching or mentorship. If you want to do something exceptionally well, you need to surround yourself with the right mentors. Anything that you'll ever do well will be the result of high-quality coaching and mentoring. If you suck at something, it's because you haven't received quality coaching in that thing. And the best coaches are paid coaching. By paying, you'll be invested, and as such, you'll listen more carefully. You'll care more. You'll be more thoughtful and engaged. There will be higher consequences for not succeeding.

If you don't pay for something, you rarely pay attention. Most people want free stuff. But if you get something for free, you rarely prize that thing. You rarely take it seriously.

Relationships

To succeed in your quest to grow and accelerate your wealth, you have to invest in fulfilling relationships. Hang out with people that will challenge you and force you to grow and do the same for others by sharing your knowledge. Remember that the quality of your accomplishments will depend on the quality of your relationships. So don't hesitate to discontinue relationships that will distract you from your ultimate life goals.

When it comes to building relationships, it is important to acknowledge that everyone is highly dependent on other people to do what they do. But it takes wisdom and humility to openly acknowledge that dependence. So you must have a mindset that will allow you to see this as a strength rather than seeing it as a weakness.

Building a fruitful relationship also requires that you constantly express your appreciation to the people in your life. That which you appreciate appreciates. Relationships are assets that can and should grow bigger and better over time. The brilliant entrepreneur Michael Fishman puts it nicely in this quote:

"Self-made is an illusion. There are many people who played divine roles in you having the life that you have today. Be sure to let them know how grateful you are."

If you don't appreciate and give to your relationships, your relationships will suffer. All relationships are like bank accounts, and if one person is constantly depositing and the other person is constantly withdrawing, eventually, all of the resources become depleted.

When investing in relationships, consider all forms of relationships. Relationships with your

- spouse
- children and parents
- employees
- customers
- suppliers
- business partners
- community members

Look for ways to give more than you receive. Have a primary motivation to give but also recognize that it is important to ask for lots of help. You should constantly be seeking and receiving help. As you continually give and receive, your relational bank account continues to grow and expand, providing several intended and unintended benefits.

Age
Assessing your age will determine how much time you have in the investment time frame and will ultimately influence the plans you develop for building and accelerating your wealth.

Age will also play a critical role in determining which of the wealth accelerator tools I discussed earlier you can employ in growing your wealth. For example, if you're seventy-one years old, you will not be able to contribute to your RRSP.

Also, when it comes to investing, you want to assess your risks based on your age. Generally speaking, the younger you are, the riskier your investment portfolio can be. The reason being that the younger a person is, the more time they have to recover and recoup any losses from things like a sudden market downturn.

When it comes to building wealth, my philosophy is always to stay invested in real assets no matter your age. So always be investing. This is our slogan:

ABI—Always Be Investing.

Action Step 4—Execute

To achieve your life goals, you must execute. To execute successfully, you must develop systems that will make execution effortless.

You need a system to execute your priorities every day. A system that will allow you to break down your decade-long goals into annual goals, then to quarterly goals, then monthly goals, then weekly goals, and, finally, to daily goals.

You are three times more likely to achieve your goals by stating your implementation intentions. You can use the

3x3 Achievement System to reach your life goals by breaking down your

- quarterly Big Three Goals
- weekly Big Three Outcomes
- daily Big Three Tasks

By doing this, you ensure that you are doing at least one thing each day toward your long-term goals. And by taking one step toward your big goals every day, you'll soon achieve your life goals.

The main reason most people don't execute well is distraction. Distractions steal your time and clutter your focus. As such, to be successful in reaching your life goals, you must be brutally focused and minimize everything that does not advance your long-term vision daily.

Staying focused can be challenging, particularly given that we often have more things to do than time to do them. So instead of figuring out how to get more done, you should be asking, "What work is the best possible use of my time?"

> *"You can do anything you want, but not everything you want."*
> *– David Allen*

So how do you do this? Here is a suggested framework:

- Regularly assess how you spend your time and energy. Do this by reviewing your calendars, writing things down, looking at devices, etc.
- Always ask yourself, "Is there a way that this contributes to my long-term goals?" If the answer is "yes," then all good. If the answer is anything other than "yes," then delegate, defer, or delete.
- Be ruthless with accomplishing your daily big three tasks as this gives you massive momentum toward your long-term goals. If you get your big three daily tasks figured out, start with the hardest task, and do nothing else until you complete it. Then move on to the next task.
- Invest in self-awareness. Spirituality, meditation, books—these things will help you figure out who you are, where you're going, why it matters, what matters, and what doesn't.

By regularly assessing how you spend your time, you may find the following as examples of things you can cut out of your life:

- People that distract you from your long-term vision
- Long meetings or meetings without an agenda
- Events/conferences and social gatherings that don't inspire and add value to your long-term vision
- Time wasted in avoidable travel time
- Social media is an addictive waste of time and energy

- Checking your messages and emails every time your phone beeps
- Picking your phone every time it rings
- Excessive addiction to news media
- Excessive use of alcohol, weed, and drugs that disrupt your sleep and negatively impact your mental state
- Doing chores you don't enjoy when you can pay others to do them
- Watching excessive TV
- Wasting too much time learning and doing tasks that someone else can do, particularly tasks you don't enjoy doing

"Never do anything that someone else can or will do, when there is so much to be done that others cannot or will not do."
– Dawson Trotman

BOOK KEN FOR A ONE-ON-ONE COACHING SESSION

If you've been working to improve your personal finance and grow your wealth tax efficiently for a while now and things aren't happening as fast as you want, then I'd like to help you create a **MAJOR BREAKTHROUGH** in your personal finances. Here's the scoop...

I've heard from many clients and professionals who are having an especially difficult time reducing taxes and growing their wealth these days. After hearing about so many people's struggles, I decided to do something about it.

** NEW, For a Limited Time **

I'd like to invite you to take advantage of a special **"Personal Financial Breakthrough"** coaching session where we'll work together to:

- Create a crystal-clear vision for your "**ultimate personal success**" and the "**perfect lifestyle**" you'd like to provide for yourself and your family.
- Uncover hidden challenges that may be sabotaging your growth and keeping you from making meaningful progress.
- Leave this session renewed, reenergized, and inspired to turn your ideas into a highly profitable, revenue-generating machine that practically runs itself.

If you'd like to take advantage of this very special, very limited, and totally FREE thirty-minute "Personal Financial Breakthrough" coaching session, click the "BOOK MY COACHING" button below:

BOOK MY COACHING
www.plantoretirewell.ca/coaching

Ken is the creator of PlanToRetireWell.ca, a one-of-a-kind educational platform that has been uniquely designed to offer a course on the fundamentals of successful tax-efficient wealth accumulation. In order to be a successful tax-smart Canadian, you need more information, and you need knowledge followed by action. Knowledge combines information about the past and applies it to the ever-changing environments and mindsets of the world. Having keen insights into the dynamic and uncertain future is paramount. However, it is action that unites every great success. Action is what produces results. Knowledge is only power when it comes into the hands of someone who knows how to take effective action. Ultimate power is the ability to produce the results that you desire most.

Ken Green has helped many of his clients and followers get on the right path to managing their taxes smartly and subsequently growing their wealth. If you want results, then this coaching session is for you!

ABOUT THE AUTHOR

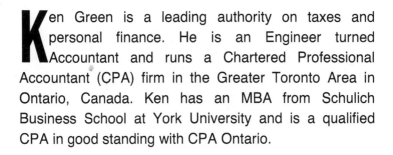

Ken Green is a leading authority on taxes and personal finance. He is an Engineer turned Accountant and runs a Chartered Professional Accountant (CPA) firm in the Greater Toronto Area in Ontario, Canada. Ken has an MBA from Schulich Business School at York University and is a qualified CPA in good standing with CPA Ontario.

Ken is an author and a regular contributor on Medium, where he shares his knowledge through his *published articles* (https://medium.com/@ken_91806). Ken works with professionals and businesses to manage their taxes. He has helped hundreds of clients through his tax and business advisory services.

Recently, Ken created PlanToRetireWell.ca and uses this platform to educate clients and to coach them to achieve breakthrough in their personal finance and businesses. He is on a mission to get every Canadian to take meaningful action to achieve financial freedom.

Ken volunteers his time serving in his church and in the community. He founded the Oakville Chess Club, Chess for Community, and Elevate My Chess Canada and uses these platforms to teach and promote the benefits of chess education in our community. He lives in Oakville, Ontario and worships at Hope Bible Church in Oakville with his family. Ken is married to Marie, and they are blessed with three children—John, Hallie, and Adiel.

THANK YOU !

Thank You For Reading My Book!

I really appreciate all of your feedback, and I love hearing what you have to say.

I need your input to make the next version of this book and my future books even better.

Please leave me a helpful review on Amazon letting me know what you thought of the book.

Also, I invite you to join the **<u>Tax-Efficient Wealth by Ken Green Facebook Group</u>** for additional insights to help you implement the ideas in this book.

Thank you so much!
Ken Green, CPA CA, MBA

Made in the USA
Columbia, SC
30 October 2020